NEW SONGS FOR CHILDREN

Easy piano arrangements of famous songs which will always appeal to c[hildren].
Printed with full words, guitar boxes and chord symbols.

Wise Publications
London/New York/Paris/Sydney/Copenhagen/Madrid

This publication is not authorised for sale in the United States of America and/or Canada.

Exclusive Distributors:
Music Sales Limited
8/9 Frith Street, London W1V 5TZ, England.

Music Sales Pty Limited
120 Rothschild Avenue, Rosebery, NSW 2018, Australia.

Order No. AM13798
ISBN 0-86001-051-1
This book © Copyright 1982, 1995 by Wise Publications

Unauthorised reproduction of any part
of this publication by any means including
photocopying is an infringement of copyright.

Book design by John Gorham
Compiled by Peter Lavender

Printed in the United Kingdom by
J.B. Offset Printers (Marks Tey) Limited, Marks Tey, Essex.

Your Guarantee of Quality
As publishers, we strive to produce every book to the highest commercial standards.
This book has been carefully designed to minimise awkward page turns and to make playing
from it a real pleasure. Particular care has been given to specifying acid-free, neutral-sized
paper made from pulps which have not been elemental chlorine bleached.
This pulp is from farmed sustainable forests and was produced with special regard
for the environment. Throughout, the printing and binding have been planned to ensure
a sturdy, attractive publication which should give years of enjoyment.
If your copy fails to meet our high standards, please inform us and we will gladly replace it.

Music Sales' complete catalogue describes thousands of titles and is available in full colour sections by
subject, direct from Music Sales Limited. Please state your areas of interest and send a cheque/postal order
for £1.50 for postage to: Music Sales Limited, Newmarket Road, Bury St. Edmunds, Suffolk IP33 3YB.

Visit the Internet Music Shop at
http://www.musicsales.co.uk

Contents

A Windmill In Old Amsterdam 10
Amazing Grace 4
Consider Yourself 6
England Swings 13
English Country Garden 16
Food Glorious Food 18
Going To The Zoo 22
If I Had A Hammer 24
Little White Duck 42
Mockin' Bird Hill 26
Morning Has Broken 28
Ob-La-Di, Ob-La-Da 32
The Candy Man 37
The Marvellous Toy 46
The Queen's Highway 44
The Unicorn 49
Three Wheels On My Wagon 52
When You Come To The End Of A Lollipop 55
Yellow Submarine 58
You're A Pink Toothbrush 62

AMAZING GRACE

TRADITIONAL, ADAPTED BY JUDY COLLINS

© Copyright 1970 by Rocky Mountain National Park Music Company Incorporated New York, USA.
All rights for the British Commonwealth of Nations (excluding Canada) and the Republic of Eire
controlled by Harmony Music Limited, 1A Farm Place, London W8.
All Rights Reserved. International Copyright Secured.

3. man - y dan - gers toils and snares, we
4. we've been there ten thou - sand years, Bright
F Bb F
have al - read - y come 'Twas grace that
shi - ning as the sun We've no less
F C7 F
brought us safe thus far and grace will lead us
days to sing Gods praise than when we first be -
F7 Bb F C7
2nd time D.S. al Coda
home. 4. When
gun. 5. Am -
F
CODA
see.
Bb F

CONSIDER YOURSELF
WORDS & MUSIC BY LIONEL BART

Moderato

Con-sid-er your-self at home, Con-sid-er your-self one of the fam-i-ly, We've tak-en to you so strong, It's clear we're go-ing to get a-long! Con-

©Copyright 1959 by Lakeview Music Publishing Company Limited, London W1.
All Rights Reserved. International Copyright Secured.

sid-er your-self well in: con - sid-er your-self part of the fur-ni-ture. There is-n't a lot to spare: Who cares? What-ev-er we've got we share!

If it should chance to be we should see some hard-er days,
No-bo-dy tries to be lah-di-dah and up-pit-y,

Emp - ty lar - der days. _____ Why grouse? _____
There's a cup of tea _____ for all. _____

Al - ways a chance we'll meet some - bod - y to foot the bill, _____
On - ly it's wise to be han - dy wiv a roll - ing pin, _____

Then the drinks are on the house! _____
When the land - lord comes to call! _____ } Con -

sid - der your - self _____ our mate, _____ We

don't want to have ____ no fuss, ____ For aft-er some con-sid-er-a-tion, We can state con-sid-er your-self ____ one of us. Con-sid-er your-self ____ one of us. ____

A WINDMILL IN OLD AMSTERDAM

WORDS & MUSIC BY TED DICKS & MYLES RUDGE

A mouse lived in a wind-mill in old Am-ster-dam
mouse he got lone-some he took him a
First they had trip-lets and then they had
daught-ers got marr-ied and so did the

dam A wind-mill with a mouse in and he was-n't
wife A wind-mill with mice in is hard-ly sur-
quins A wind-mill with quins in trip-lets and
sons The wind-mill had christ-'nings when no - one was

grous-ing. He sang ev-'ry morn-ing "How luck-y I am
pris-in'. She sang ev-'ry morn-ing "How luck-y I am
twins in. They sang ev-'ry morn-ing "How luck-y we are
list-'nin'. They all sang in chor-us "How luck-y we am

© Copyright 1964 Westminster Music Limited,
Suite 2.07, Plaza 535 Kings Road, London SW10.
All Rights Reserved. International Copyright Secured.

liv - ing in a wind - mill in old Am - ster - dam."
liv - ing in a wind - mill in old Am - ster - dam."
liv - ing in a wind - mill in Am - ster - dam ya."
liv - ing in a wind - mill in old Am - ster - dam."

Db   Gb   C7   Bb

I saw a mouse Where? There on a stair. Where on a stair? Right there, a lit - tle mouse with clogs on, Well I de -

F   Bb   F   C7   F   F   Bb   F

clare go - ing clip clip - pe - ty clop on the stair Oh yeah

2. The
3. -
4. The
Coda. A

Last time to Coda

CODA

mouse lived in a wind - mill so snug and so nice There's no - bo - dy there now but a whole lot of mice.

rit.

ENGLAND SWINGS
WORDS & MUSIC BY ROGER MILLER

F B♭ B♭7 C7 E♭

Moderato

Now if you huff and puff and you fin-'lly save e-nough mo-ney
up to take your fa-mi-ly on a trip a-cross the sea
Take a tip be-fore you take your trip, Let me tell you
where to go, go to En-ge-land. ___ Oh

© Copyright 1965 by Tree Publishing Co. Inc. USA.
All rights for the world (ex USA & Canada) controlled by Burlington Music Company Limited.
All Rights Reserved. International Copyright Secured.

CHORUS

En-ge-land swings like a pen-du-lum do, Bob-bies on bi-cy-cles two by two, West-min-ster Ab-bey, the tow'r of Big Ben, the ro-sy red cheeks of the lit-tle child-ren

to Coda

VERSE 2

Ma-ma's old pa-ja-mas and your Pa-pa's must-ache,

Fall-ing out the win-dow sill fro-lic in the grass

Tryin' to mock the way they talk fun, but all in vain

Gap-ing at the dap-per men with Der-by hats and canes.

D.S. al Coda

CODA

(Whistle)

ENGLISH COUNTRY GARDEN
WORDS & MUSIC BY ROBERT M. JORDAN

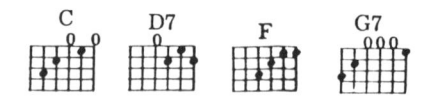

Moderato

1. How many gentle flowers grow in an English Country Garden.
2. How many insects find their home in an English Country Garden.
3. How many songbirds make their nests in an English Country Garden.

I'll tell you now of some I know and those I miss, I hope you'll pardon.

Daf-fo-dils, hearts-ease and flocks, Meadow sweet and lilies, stocks,
Dragon flies, moths and bees, Spiders falling from the trees,
Bab-le-ing coo-cooing doves, Robins and the warbling thrush,

© 1958 & 1972 Tin Pan Alley Music Company Limited,
8 Serviden Drive, Bromley, Kent.
All Rights Reserved. International Copyright Secured.

gen - tle lu - pin and tall hol - ly - hocks, Ros - es
but - ter - flies sway in the mild gen - tle breeze, There are
blue - bird, lark, finch and night - in - gale, We all

fox - gloves snow - drops, For - get - me - nots, In an
hedge - hogs that roam, And lit - tle gnomes, In an
smile in the spring when the birds all start to sing, In an

Eng - lish Coun - try Gar - den.

FOOD GLORIOUS FOOD
WORDS & MUSIC BY LIONEL BART

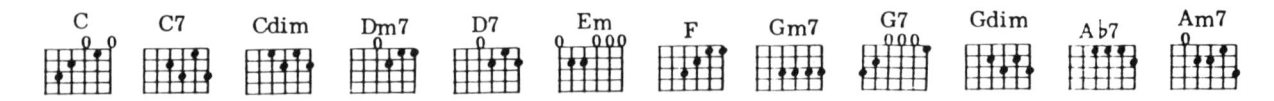

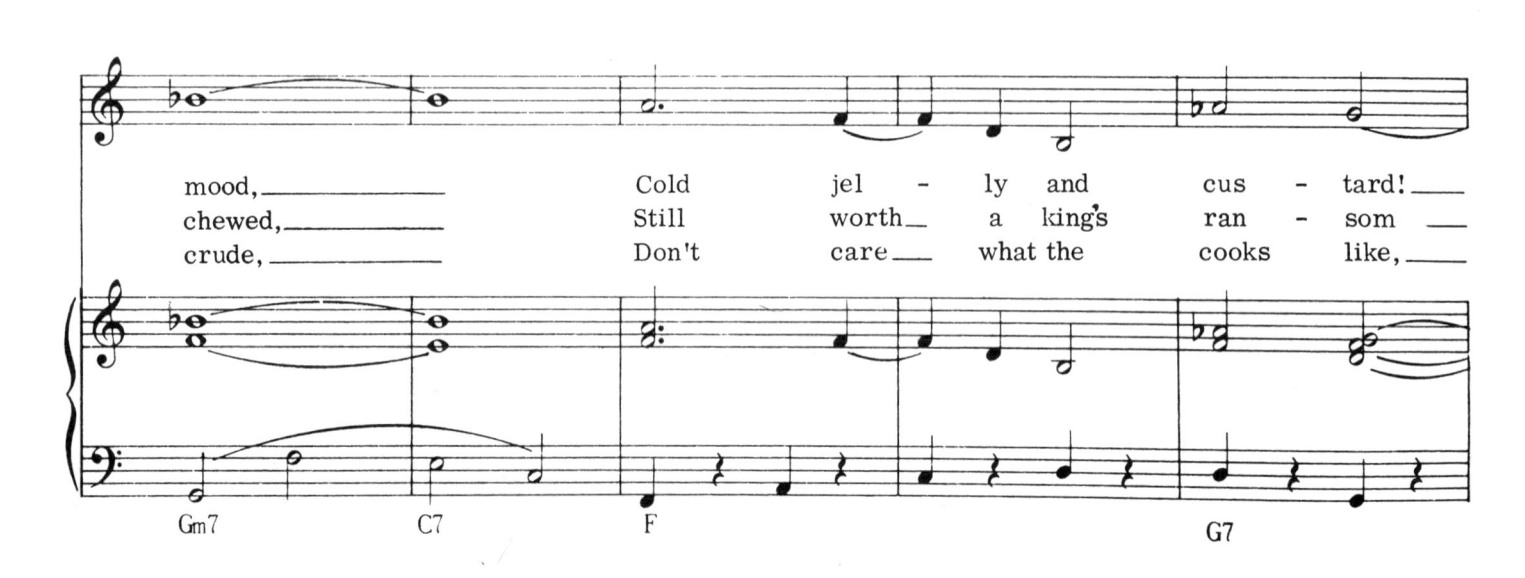

CHORUS

Brightly in 2

1. Food glor - i - ous food! _____ Hot saus-
2. Food glor - i - ous food! _____ What is
3. Food glor - i - ous food! _____ Don't care

- age and mus - tard! _____ While we're in the
- there more hand - some? _____ Gulped, swal - lowed or
- what it looks like, _____ Burned, un - der - done,

mood, _____ Cold jel - ly and cus - tard! _____
chewed, _____ Still worth a king's ran - som _____
crude, _____ Don't care what the cooks like, _____

© Copyright 1959 by Lakeview Music Publishing Company Limited, London W1.
All Rights Reserved. International Copyright Secured.

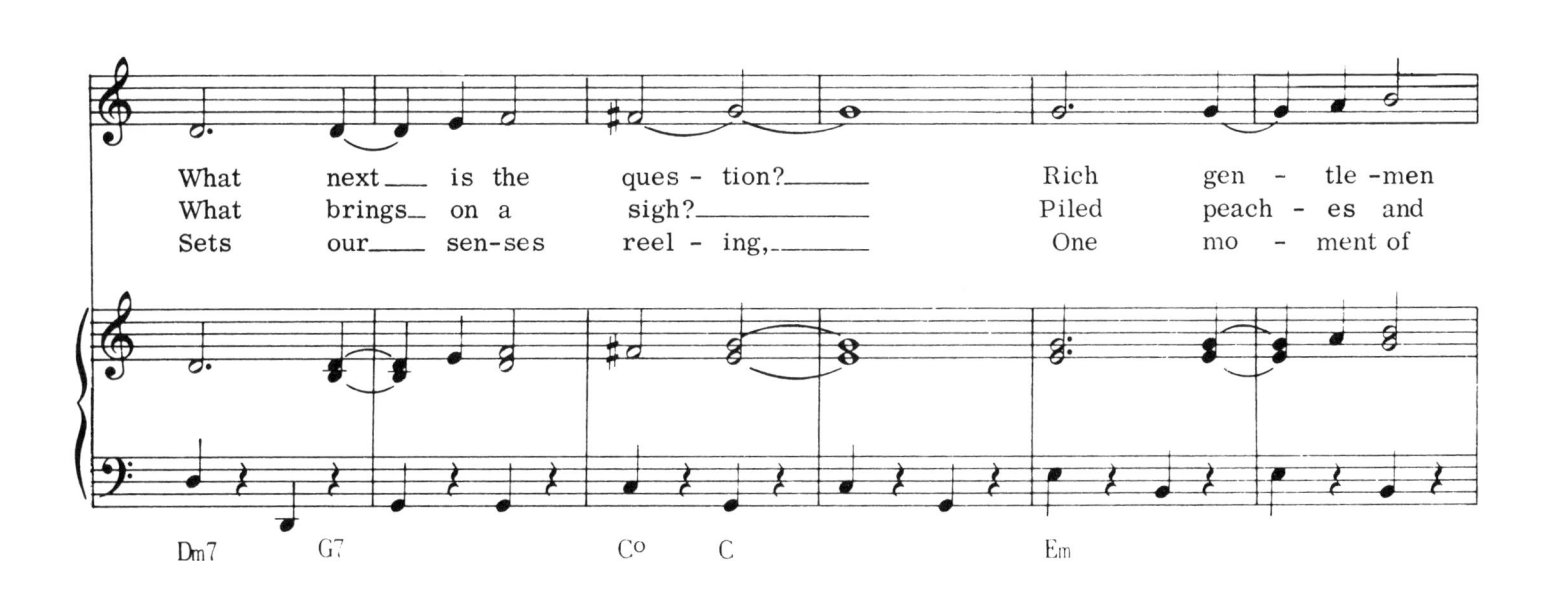

pease pud - ding and sav - el - oys, __
what is __ it we dream a - bout, __
just think - ing of grow - ing fat, __

What next __ is the ques - tion? __ Rich gen - tle - men
What brings __ on a sigh? __ Piled peach - es and
Sets our __ sen - ses reel - ing, __ One mo - ment of

have it boys in - dye - ges - tion! __
cream, a - bout six - feet high! __
know - ing that full - up feel - ing! __

Food glor - i - ous food! We're anx-
Food glor - i - ous food! Eat right
Food glor - i - ous food! What would-
C Gm7 C7 F
ious to try it. Three ban - quets a
through the men - u Just loos - en your
n't we give for, That ex - tra bit
G7 C
day, Our fav - our-ite di - et!
belt, Two in - ches and then you
more, That's all that we live for,
Gm7 C7 F G7
Just pic - ture a great big steak.
Work up a new ap - pe - tite.
Why should we be fat - ed too?
C G° Dm7 G7

Fried, roast-ed or stewed. Oh, food, won-der-ful
In this in-ter-lude. Then, food, once a-gain
Do no-thing but brood. On, food, mag-ic-al

Am7   D7   Ab7   C   Am7

food, Mar-vel-lous food, Glor-i-ous food!
food, Fa-bu-lous food, Glor-i-ous food!
food, Mag-ic-al

D7   G7   C   G7

food, Mar-vel-lous food, Fa-bu-lous food, beau-

C   Am7   D7   G7

-ti-ful food, Glor-i-ous food!

C

Going to the Zoo

WORDS & MUSIC BY TOM PAXTON

Daddy's taking us to the zoo tomorrow, zoo tomorrow, zoo tomorrow, Daddy's taking us to the zoo tomorrow, we can stay all day. We're going to the zoo, zoo, zoo, how about you, you, you? You can come too, too, too, we're go-ing to the zoo, zoo, zoo.

2. See the elephant with the long trunk swingin'
Great big ears and long trunk swingin'
Sniffin' up peanuts with the long trunk swingin'
We can stay all day.
(Chorus)

3. See all the monkeys scritch, scritch, scratchin,'
Jumpin' all around and scritch, scritch, scratchin,'
Hangin' by their long tails scritch, scritch, scratchin,'
We can stay all day.
(Chorus)

4. Big black bear all huff, huff, a-puffin'
Coat's too heavy, he's huff, huff, a-puffin,'
Don't get too near the huff, huff, a-puffin,'
Or you won't stay all day.
(Chorus)

5. Seals in the pool all honk, honk, honkin,'
Catchin' fish and honk, honk, honkin,'
Little seals honk, honk, honkin,' (high pitched voice)
We can stay all day.
(Chorus)

6. (Slower Tempo)
We stayed all day and I'm gettin' sleepy,
Sittin' in the car gettin' sleep, sleep, sleepy,
Home already and I'm sleep, sleep, sleepy,
We have stayed all day.
(Chorus)

7. Mamma's taking us to the zoo tomorrow, zoo tomorrow, zoo tomorrow,
Mamma's taking us to the zoo tomorrow;
We can stay all day.

Chorus:
We've been to the zoo, zoo, zoo,
So have you, you, you,
You came too, too, too,
We've been to the zoo, zoo, zoo,

IF I HAD A HAMMER

WORDS & MUSIC BY LEE HAYS & PETE SEEGER

© Copyright 1958 and 1959 by Ludlow Music Inc. New York, USA.
Assigned to TRO Essex Music Limited for the territory of the British Commonwealth of Nations
excluding Canada also the Republics of Ireland and South Africa.
All Rights Reserved. International Copyright Secured.

dan - ger, — I'd ham-mer out a warn - ing, —
dan - ger, — I'd ring out a warn - ing, —
dan - ger, — I'd sing out a warn - ing, —
jus - tice, — It's the bell of free - dom, —

I'd ham-mer out love be-tween all of my broth-ers,
I'd ring out love be-tween all of my broth-ers,
I'd sing out love be-tween all of my broth-ers,
It's the song a-bout love be-tween broth-ers and sist-ers,

All _____ o - ver this land. _____

2. If I had a
3. If I had a
4. Well I got a land. _____

MOCKIN' BIRD HILL

WORDS & MUSIC BY VAUGHN HORTON

Bright tempo

1. When the sun in the mornin' peeps over the hill and kisses the roses round my window sill; Then my heart fills with gladness when I hear the trill of the birds in the tree tops on Mockin'-bird Hill.

2. three cornered plough and an acre to till and a mule that I bought for a ten dollar bill; There's a tumble down shack and a rusty ol' mill, but it's my home sweet home up on Mockin'-bird Hill.

3. late in the evening I climb up the hill and survey all my kingdom while everything's still; only me and the sky and an ol' whip-poor-will singin' songs in the twilight on Mockin'-bird Hill.

© Copyright 1949 Southern Music Publishing Company Incorporated, USA.
Peermusic (UK) Limited, 8-14 Verulam Street, London WC1.
All Rights Reserved. International Copyright Secured.

CHORUS

Tra-la la twit-tle dee dee dee, It gives me a thrill to wake up in the morn-in' to the mock-in' birds trill; Tra-la la twit-tle dee dee dee, There's peace and good will; You're wel-come as the flow-ers on Mock-in'-bird Hill.

2. Got a
3. When it's Hill.

MORNING HAS BROKEN

WORDS BY ELEANOR FARJEON
MUSIC BY CAT STEVENS

© Copyright 1971 Cat Music Limited. Administered for the World by
Westbury Music Consultants Limited, 56 Wigmore Street, London W1H 9DG.
All Rights Reserved. International Copyright Secured.

Praise for them spring - ing fresh from ___ the world.
Sprung in com - plete - ness where His ___ feet pass.

3. Mine is the sun-light, Mine is the morn - - ing, Born of the one light E - den saw play. Praise with e - la - tion, Praise ev - 'ry morn - ing,

God's re - cre - a - tion of the new day.

OB-LA-DI, OB-LA-DA
WORDS & MUSIC BY JOHN LENNON & PAUL McCARTNEY

Bright tempo

VERSES

Desmond has a barrow in the market place, Molly is the singer in a band. Desmond says to Molly "Girl I like your face" And Molly

© Copyright 1968 Northern Songs.
All Rights Reserved. International Copyright Secured.

says this as she takes him by the hand, Ob - la - di
G D7 G
ob la da, Life goes on, Bra -
G Bm
la la, How the life goes on.
Em G D7
Ob - la - di ob - la - da
G

Life goes on, Bra - la - la, How the life goes on.
to Coda
In a cou-ple of years they have built a home sweet home.
G
Bm
Em
G
D7
G
1
2
G
C
G

With a cou-ple of kids run-ning in the yard _____ Of Des-mond and Mol-ly Jones. _____

D.S. al Segno

CODA

And if you want some fun _____

Take Ob - la - di - bla - da.

2. Desmond takes a trolley to the jeweller's stores
Buys a twenty carat golden ring
Takes it back to Molly waiting at the door
And as he gives it to her she begins to sing.

3. Happy ever after in the market place
Desmond lets the children lend a hand
Molly stays at home and does her pretty face
And in the evening she still sings it with the band.

THE CANDY MAN

WORDS & MUSIC BY LESLIE BRICUSSE & ANTHONY NEWLEY

Ad lib. (not too slowly)

VERSE

I can't stop eating sweets! All those wonderful
Willy Wonka treats. You can keep the others, 'cause
me, I'm a Wonker-er. When it comes to
candy, Willy's the conqueror.

p colla voce

A little slower

a tempo

rall.

© Copyright 1970 & 1971 by Taradam Music Incorporated, USA.
BMG Music Publishing Limited, Bedford House, 69-79 Fulham High Street, London SW6.
This arrangement © 1995 BMG Music Publishing Limited.
All Rights Reserved. International Copyright Secured.

REFRAIN
Moderato, Joyfully

Who can take a sun-rise sprin-kle it with dew,
Who can take a rain-bow wrap it in a sigh,

cov-er it in choc-'late and a mir-a-cle or two? The
soak it in the sun and make a straw-b'ry lem-on pie?

can-dy man, (The can-dy man, the can-dy man can. the can-dy man can.) The can-dy man can 'cause he mix - es it with love and makes the world taste good.

Dm7 C G7

2 world taste good. The can-dy man makes ev-'ry-thing he bakes

C F F#°

sat - is - fy - ing and de - li - cious. Talk a - bout your child - hood

C B7

wish - es. You can e - ven eat the dish - es.

Em Dm7 G7

Who can take to-mor-row,
Dm7 G7 C A7
dip it in a dream,
sep-a-rate the sor-row and col-
Dm7 G7 C F
lect up all the cream? The can-dy man,
(The can-dy man, the
can-dy man can. the can-dy man can.)
E7 Am7 Am7 D7 Dm7 G7
The can-dy man can 'cause he
C Am7 D7

1
mix - es it with love and makes the world_ taste good.
The
G7
C
2
Very slowly ad lib.
world_ taste good.
And the world tastes good 'cause the
p
mp
C
Am7
D7
Moderato
can - dy man thinks_ it should.
rall.
Dm7
Bb
C
Repeat and fade out
mp
dim. poco a poco
Bb
C

THE LITTLE WHITE DUCK
WORDS BY WALT BARROWS. MUSIC BY BERNARD ZARITZKY

Brightly

1. There's a little white duck sitting in the water A little white duck Doing what he oughter, He took a bite of a lily pad Flapped his wings and he said, "I'm glad I'm a little white duck sitting in the water"

2. (There's a) little green frog swimming in the water A little green frog Doing what he oughter, He jumped right off of the lily pad That the little duck bit and he said, "I'm glad I'm a little green frog swimming in the water"

© Copyright 1950 General Music Publishing Company Incorporated, USA.
Peermusic (UK) Limited, 8-14 Verulam Street, London WC1.
All Rights Reserved. International Copyright Secured.

3. (There's a) Little black bug floating in the water,
A little black bug doing what he oughter,
He tickled the frog on the lily pad,
That the little duck bit and he said,
"I'm glad I'm a little black bug floating on the water,"
chirp, chirp, chirp.

4. (There's a) Little red snake lying in the water,
Little red snake doing what he oughter,
He frightened the duck and the frog so bad,
Hit the little bug and he said,
"I'm glad I'm a little red snake lying in the water,"
sss, sss, sss.

5. (Now there's) Nobody left sitting in the water,
Nobody left doing what he oughter,
There's nothing left but the lily pad, The duck and the frog ran away it's sad
That there's nobody left sitting in the water
Boo, hoo, hoo.

THE QUEEN'S HIGHWAY
WORDS & MUSIC BY TOMMIE CONNOR & JOHNNY REINE

Marcato

We must have safe-ty on the Queen's High-way First halt look right, look left, then look right a-gain then off we go if the road is clear Safe-ly home to mum-my 'cos there's no-thing to fear.

© Copyright 1953 Peermusic (UK) Limited,
8-14 Verulam Street, London WC1.
All Rights Reserved. International Copyright Secured.

Don't be in a hurry going to and fro the school
Halt at ev-'ry crossing, do your safety drill and then
Kerb drill for you is the golden rule.
You'll make your way safely home again.
We must have safety on the Queen's Highway, So
1. let's start from today. We
2. -day.

THE MARVELLOUS TOY
WORDS & MUSIC BY TOM PAXTON

When I was just a wee little lad, Full of health and joy, My Father homeward came one night, And gave to me a toy. A wonder to behold it was, With many colours

© Copyright 1961 Cherry Lane Music Company Incorporated.
Assigned to Harmony Music Limited, 1A Farm Place, London W8 for the British Commonwealth (excluding Canada),
the Republics of Eire and South Africa.
All Rights Reserved. International Copyright Secured.

bright, And the mo-ment I laid eyes on it, It be-came my heart's de-light. It went "Zip" when it moved, And "Bop" when it stopped, And "Whirr" when it stood still. I nev-er knew just what it was, And I guess I nev-er will.

D.C.

The first time that I picked it up I had a big surprise,
For right on its bottom were two big buttons that looked like big green eyes,
I first pushed one and then the other, and then I twisted its lid,
And when I set it down again, this is what it did.

It first marched left and then marched right and then marched under a chair,
And when I looked where it had gone, it wasn't even there!
I started to sob and my daddy laughed, for he knew what I would find,
When I turned around, my marvellous toy, chugging from behind.

Well, the years have gone by too quickly, it seems, I have my own little boy,
And yesterday I gave to him my marvellous little toy,
His eyes nearly popped right out of his head and he gave a squeal of glee,
Neither one of us knows just what it is, but he loves it, just like me.

Last Chorus:
It still goes 'Zip' when it moves and 'Bop' when it stops,
And 'Whirr' when it stands still,
I never knew just what it was,
And I guess I never will.

THE UNICORN
WORDS & MUSIC BY SHEL SILVERSTEIN

Chords: F F7 B♭ C7

Moderately slow

1. A long time a-go when the earth was green, there was more kinds of an-i-mals then you've ev-er seen. And they'd run a-round free while the world was be-ing born, And the love-li-est of all was the u-ni-corn.

© Copyright 1962 and 1968 by Hollis Music Inc. New York, USA.
All rights for the British Commonwealth of Nations (ex Canada and Australasia)
and the Republic of Eire controlled by TRO Essex Music Limited.
All Rights Reserved. International Copyright Secured.

CHORUS

There was green al-li-ga-tors and long necked geese,
Hump back cam-els and chim-pan-zees, Cats and rats and e-le-phants but
sure as you're born, The love-li-est of all was the u-ni-corn.

2. But the

u - ni - corn.

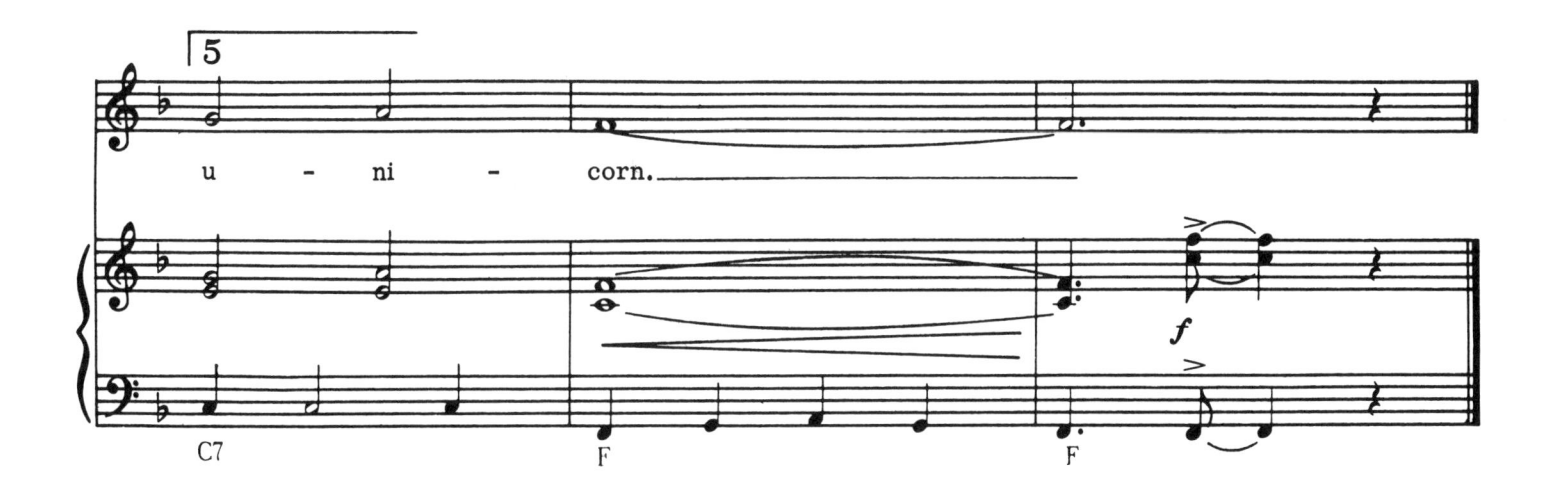

2. But the Lord seen some sinnin' and it caused Him pain,
He says "Stand back, I'm gonna make it rain,
So hey, Brother Noah, I'll tell you what to do,
Go and build me a floating zoo.

Chorus: · And you take two alligators and a couple of geese,
Two hump back camels and two chimpanzees,
Two cats, two rats, two elephants, but sure as you're born,
Noah don't you forget my unicorns."

3. Now Noah was there and he answered the callin,'
And he finished up the ark as the rain started fallin,'
Then he marched in the animals two by two,
And he sung out as they went through.

Chorus: Hey Lord, I got two alligators and a couple of geese,
Two hump back camels and two chimpanzees,
Two cats, two rats, two elephants, but sure as you're born,
Lord, I just don't see your unicorns."

4. Well, Noah looked out through the drivin' rain,
But the unicorns was hidin' playin' silly games,
They were kickin' and a splashin' while the rain was pourin,'
Oh them foolish unicorns.

Chorus: "And you take two alligators and a couple of geese,
Two hump back camels and two chimpanzees,
Two cats, two rats, two elephants, but sure as you're born,
Noah don't you forget my unicorns."

5. Then the ducks started duckin' and the snakes started snakin'
And the elephants started elephantin' and the boat started shakin'
The mice started squeakin' and the lions started roarin,'
And everyone's aboard but them unicorns.

Chorus: I mean the two alligators and the couple of geese,
The hump back camels and the chimpanzees,
Noah cried, "Close the door 'cause the rain is pourin,'
And we just can't wait for them unicorns."

6. And then the ark started movin' and it drifted with the tide,
And the unicorns looked up from the rock and cried,
And the water came up and sort of floated them away.
That's why you've never seen a unicorn to this day.

Chorus: You'll see a lot of alligators and a whole mass of geese,
You'll see hump back camels and chimpanzees,
You'll see cats and rats and elephants but sure as you're born,
You're never gonna see no unicorn.

THREE WHEELS ON MY WAGON

WORDS BY BOB HILLIARD
MUSIC BY BURT BACHARACH

Moderato

Three wheels on my wag-on, And I'm still roll-in' a-long
Two wheels on my wag-on, And I'm still roll-in' a-long
One wheel on my wag-on, And I'm still roll-in' a-long

The cher-o-kees are chas-in' me
Them cher-o-kees are af-ter me
Them cher-o-kees are af-ter me I'm

ar-rows fly right on by but I'm sing-in' a
flam-ing spears burn my ears but I'm sing-in' a
all in flames at the reins but I'm sing-in' a

hap-py song. I'm sing-in'

© Copyright 1961 Shapiro Bernstein & Company Incorporated, USA.
Shapiro Bernstein & Company Limited, 8/9 Frith Street, London W1 licensee
for British Commonwealth & Eire (excluding Canada & Australia).
All Rights Reserved. International Copyright Secured.

higety hagety Hoggety high Pi-o-neers they never say die A mile up the road there's a hidden cave And we can
never say die Half a mile up the road there's a hidden cave And we can
never say die On the very next turn there's a hidden cave And we can
watch those cherokees go galloping by.

No wheels on my wag-on So I'm not roll-in' a long The cher-o-kees have cap-tured me they look mad, Things look bad but I'm sing-in' a hap-py song. (spoken) Come on all you cherokees, sing along with me

Hig-ge-ty hag-get-y hog-get-y high pi-o-neers they nev-er say die.

repeat and fade....

WHEN YOU COME TO THE END OF A LOLLIPOP
WORDS & MUSIC BY AL HOFFMAN & DICK MANNING

Moderate waltz tempo

When you come to the end of a lol-li-pop.

To the end, To the end of a lol-li-pop,

When you come to the end of a lol-li-pop.

Plop goes your heart

© Copyright 1960 Topper Music Publishing Corporation.
Copyright 1960 Rogers Music Limited, London.
Campbell Connelly & Company Limited, 8/9 Frith Street, London W1.
All Rights Reserved. International Copyright Secured.

Gil - ly - o, Gil - ly - o, I love my lol - ly - o!

1. Down to the ve - ry last lick. But
2. Win - ter and sum - mer and spring. But

what can you do with it when you are thro' with it?
when you are done it's a - bout as much fun as a

All you have left is the stick! When you
yo - yo with - out an - y string!

come to the end of a lol-li-pop, To the
C G7 C
end, To the end of a lol-li-pop, When you
C♯o Dm7 G7
come to the end of a lol-li-pop, Plop!
fz
Dm7 G7 C C♯o Dm7
1 2
goes your heart. heart.
mf
R.H.
G7 C C G7 C

YELLOW SUBMARINE
WORDS & MUSIC BY JOHN LENNON & PAUL McCARTNEY

green And we lived ___ be-neath the waves in our
D G D C G Em
Yel - low Sub - ma - rine
Am D
We all live in a
G
Yel - low Sub-ma-rine Yel-low Sub-ma-rine Yel-low Sub-ma - rine
D G
to Coda
We all live in a Yel - low Sub - ma-rine Yel - low Sub - ma-rine
D

Yel - low Sub - ma-rine And our friends are all a -
As we live a life of
G D C
board Ma - ny more of them live next
ease Ev - 'ry one of us has all we
G Em Am
door And the band be - gins to
need Sky of blue and sea of
D G D C
1
play
Solo
3
3
G Em Am D G

2
green In our Yel - low Sub - ma - rine
D.S. al Coda
G Em Am D
CODA
Fade 2nd time
Yel - low Sub - ma - rine We all live in a
G
Yel - low Sub-ma-rine Yel - low Sub - ma-rine Yel-low Sub - ma-rine
D G
We all live in a Yel - low Sub - ma - rine Yel - low Sub - ma - rine.
D

YOU'RE A PINK TOOTHBRUSH
WORDS & MUSIC BY RALPH RUVIN, BOB HALFIN & HAROLD IRVING

You're a pink tooth-brush, I'm a blue tooth-brush, Have we met some-where be-fore? You're a pink tooth-brush, And I think tooth-brush that we met by the bath-room door, Glad to meet tooth-brush, Such a sweet tooth-brush, How you

© Copyright 1953 Sydney Bron Music Company Limited,
127 Charing Cross Road, London WC2.
All Rights Reserved. International Copyright Secured.

thrill me thru' and thru', Don't be hard tooth-brush, On a soft tooth-brush, 'Cos I can't help lov-ing you. Ev-'ry time I hear you whist-le, (Whistle------------) It makes my ny-lon brist-le,

(Whistle--------------------------------Wolf whistle) You're a pink tooth-brush, I'm a
F7
Bb
blue tooth - brush, Won't you mar - ry me in haste, I'll be
C7
true tooth - brush, Just to you tooth - brush, When we
F7
both use the same tooth - paste. You're a -paste.
1
2
Bb
Bb
Bb